IDEAS OF NOTE

One man's philosophy
of life on Post-Its

Charles Hutton

Abrams Image, New York

Dedicated to Jeff Goldblum
(who still hasn't followed me back)

Editor: David Cashion
Designer: Devin Grosz
Production Manager: True Sims

Library of Congress Control Number: 2016946249

ISBN: 978-1-4197-2416-9

Printed and bound in China
10 9 8 7 6 5 4 3 2 1

Abrams Image books are available at special discounts when purchased in quantity for premiums and promotions as well as fundraising or educational use. Special editions can also be created to specification. For details, contact specialsales@abramsbooks.com or the address below.

ABRAMS The Art of Books
115 West 18th Street, New York, NY 10011
abramsbooks.com

INTRODUCTION

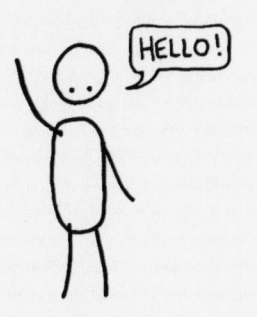

Contents

I'll start with an apology. First of all, I'm sorry to be so misleading. The subtitle of this book features the word "philosophy," but I sincerely hope you aren't hoping to be guided through life in any way. There is actually very little *good* advice to be found anywhere within these pages. There is, however, a lot of questionable advice and nonsense wrapped up in general idiocy, which is honestly far more entertaining than any good advice (that you wouldn't have listened to, anyway).

As you might be aware, this book started as an Instagram account, and like some delicate animal raised in captivity, at a certain point it got big and bad enough to warrant being released into the wilds of bookstores and Amazon pages. I sincerely hope you've discovered it gorging on the littered remains of a bigoted politician's memoir or the shredded carcass of a vlogger's book (in case you're new to this, Instagramers and YouTubers are mortal enemies). Regardless, I'm glad you got hold of this wily beast and are now doggedly dragging it by the collar, trying to get it home.

Or maybe you're not. Maybe you're just standing there, reading this in a bookstore while you wait for your partner or friend to finish whatever it is they dragged you along for. In that case, I think you've just about maxed out on the time you can read a book in a store without buying it, so pick a lane! Put this back and have a laugh at that stupid politician's book, or maybe marvel at how a video blog can make the transition into book format. Or go slam this book down on the counter and reveal yourself as someone who thoroughly enjoys lowbrow nonsense purveyed through the medium of crudely drawn comics on sticky notes.

I feel like I need to prepare you for what follows, but in reality, it's just a bunch of drawings on small pieces of paper.

I'll leave you with this thought: The intention from the very beginning, before the Instagram started, when drawing stuff like this was still a procrastination tool for me as I stared down the barrel of a nine-to-five office job, was to waste as much time as possible as 5:00 P.M. glacially approached. So I hope that the next one hundred and seventy or so pages provide ample time-wasting material for you. I hope you fail to do whole swathes of important stuff you had lined up for today, and I hope this book will inspire you to waste even more time thereafter.

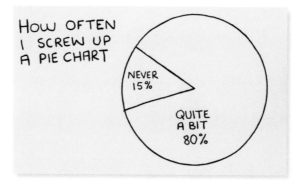

Yes, this might look like a funny, tongue-in-cheek graph, but this is deadly serious. Do you realize how many sticky notes it takes me to finally get a final sticky note drawing? I'm not going to tell you.

I thought I'd put this in so you can understand the amount of hard work that goes into drawing this kind of stuff. And yes, your suspicions are correct: You totally could have written this book.

That said, try quitting your successful architecture job by telling your employer that you've decided to draw stuff on sticky notes full time while you hope they haven't noticed that you've taped the entire office's supply of sticky notes to your body like you're a drug mule who traffics office stationery instead of drugs.

Anyway, let's do this.

WORK

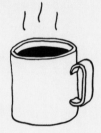

HOW TO START YOUR OWN BUSINESS
STEP ONE:
GET SOME COOL BUSINESS CARDS MADE...
CONGRATULATIONS, YOU ARE NOW A SUCCESSFUL BUSINESS OWNER.

Against all rational explanation, the distance between now and Friday actually increases the closer you get to Friday, which is about as close as you're going to get to experiencing quantum mechanics.

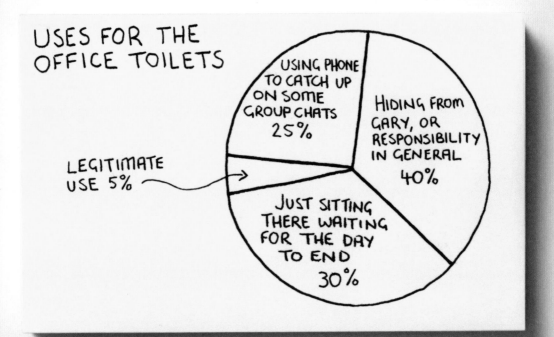

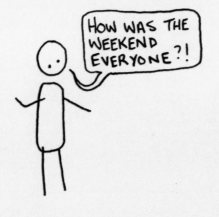
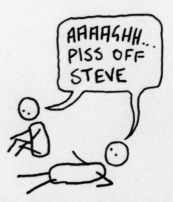

Before you engage with colleagues on a Monday, consider the following: Are you genuinely interested in what your colleague did over the weekend, or are you using that thoughtless Monday greeting because you don't have much of a connection and you're trying to eke out an engineered friendship just to be polite while you momentarily stand together in the office kitchen?

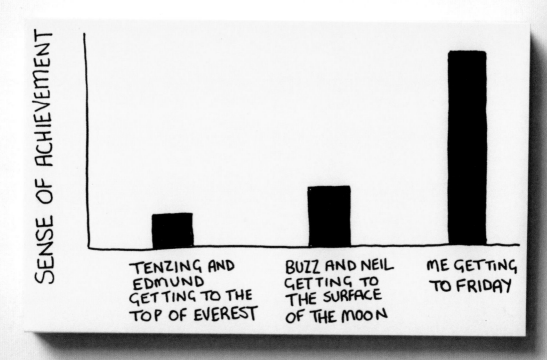

People who unthinkingly regurgitate pseudo-philosophical platitudes will tell you that you should "find something you love, and then make it your job." However, I have yet to find anyone willing to pay me to stand around completely naked and half drunk while microwaving fruit just to see what happens to it after various amounts of time.

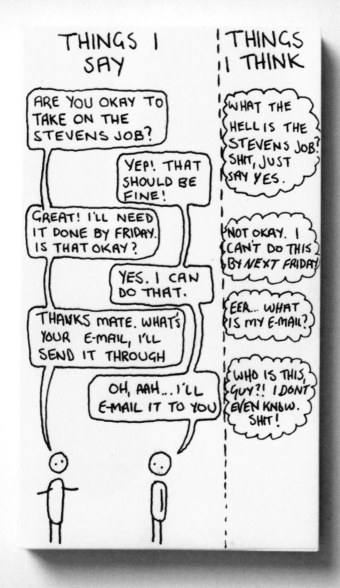

This is a visualization of the first few years of what I humorously refer to as my "professional career."

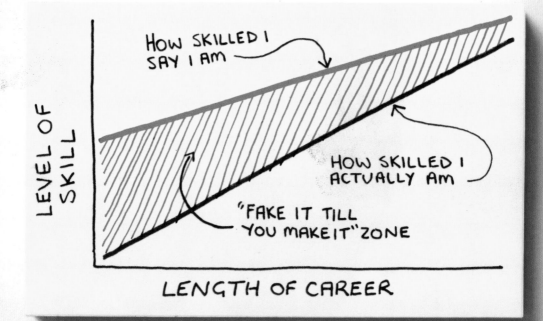

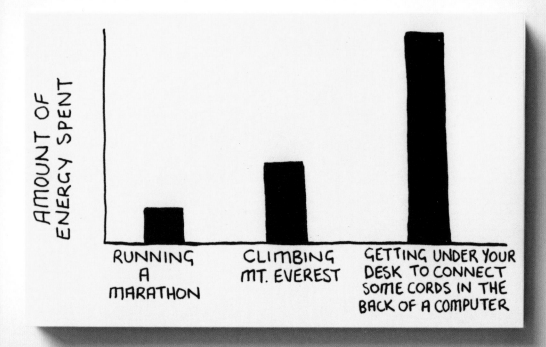

PAYDAY TO PAYDAY: A JOURNEY

WEEK 1

WEEK 2

WEEK 3

NOODLES

WEEK 4

"I deserve to celebrate and spend all my money as a reward for surviving the previous two weeks. And no, I don't care that doing so perpetuates a vicious cycle of recurring debt, because I've already had three martinis, and you're not my real dad."

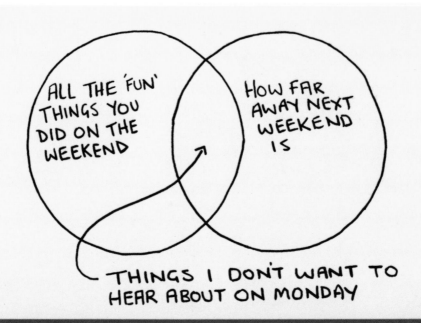

The same applies to vacations as well.

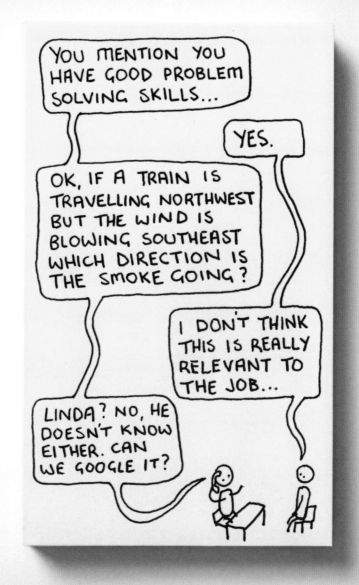

"Also, the rent in this town is astronomically high, and I should know."

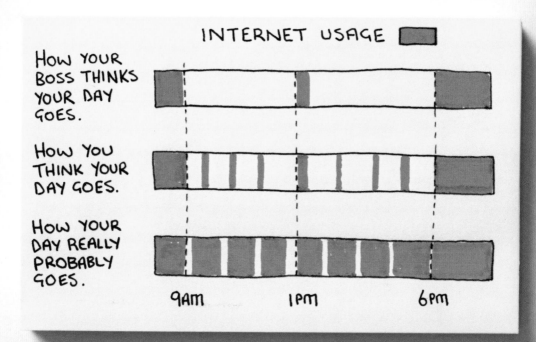

It's nearly impossible to determine whether the Internet has increased humankind's rate of innovation or actually slowed it down due to the collective number of hours we've lost to cat videos.

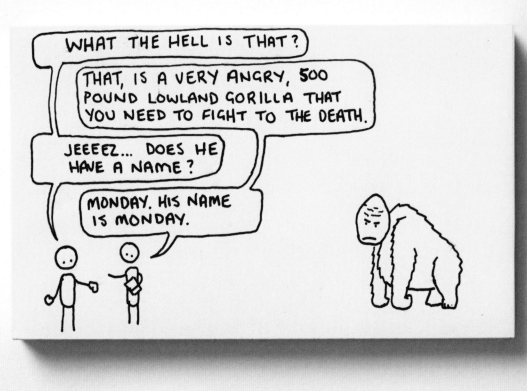

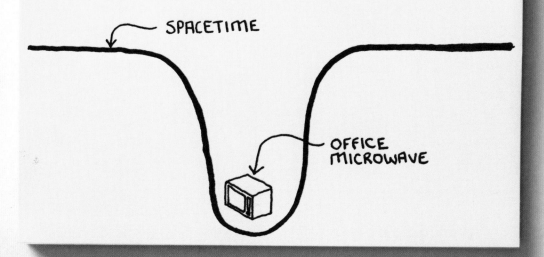

THE PHYSICS BEHIND 'WAITING FOR THE OFFICE MICROWAVE'

SPACETIME

OFFICE MICROWAVE

Newton, Einstein, Hawking. All of them missed this key concept in the area of astrophysics and space-time: If you put enough microwaves in an office kitchen, you'll slow time to a standstill while you stare into the abyss that is Linda's leftover Indian takeout, slowly reheating for eternity.

If you're going to have a fire drill, do it properly and set the building on fire. Make that thing realistic.

WOOO! IT'S FRIDAY! YOU EXCITED?!
ANY EXCITEMENT FOR 'FRIDAY' ONLY PROVES THAT YOU'RE AN UNWITTING SLAVE TO THIS SOCIAL CONSTRUCT WE CALL 'THE WEEK'. FRIDAY IS NOTHING BUT A FALSE HOPE, DESIGNED TO DISTRACT YOU FROM NOTICING THE MACHINE SILENTLY OPPRESSING YOU. YOU'RE JUST A HAMSTER ON A WHEEL LINDA, TOO EXCITED BY 'FRIDAY' TO NOTICE YOU'RE IN A CAGE.
THIS IS WHY NOBODY LIKES YOU STEVE.

HOME

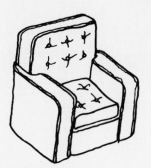

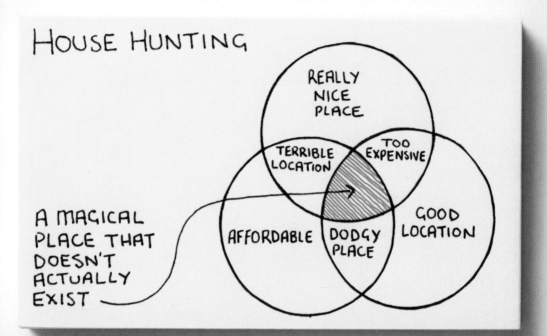

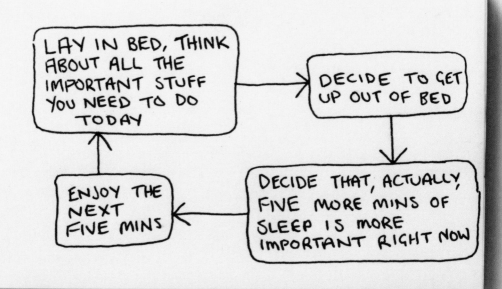

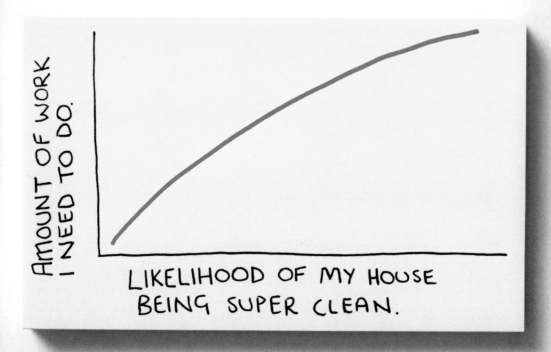

I wonder what cleaners do to procrastinate.

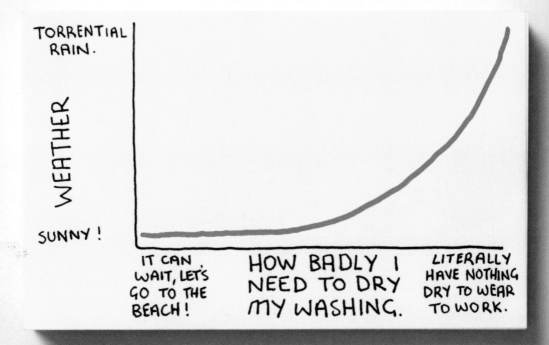

If there's ever a drought, the entire population should just get together and start doing their laundry at the same time, then sit back and watch the clouds magically roll in as a million washing machines across the country collectively hit their spin cycles.

Ideally, I'd like a house with large windows that the sun can shine through and under which I can position a couch, thereby gaining the benefits of the "amazing day" my friend's text message claims is happening outside my front door, but without having to leave the house.

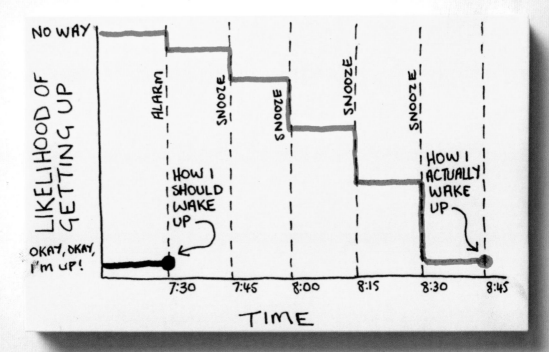

The entire world seems to have the same attitude toward dealing with climate change. Sure, we should do something—in a little bit.

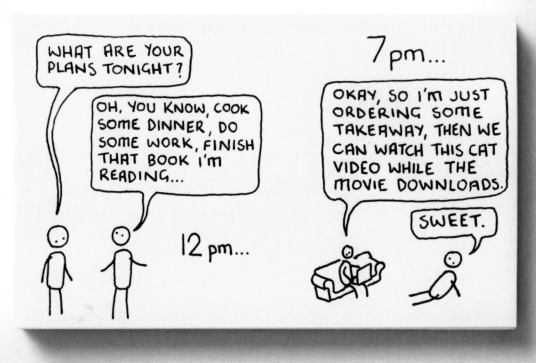

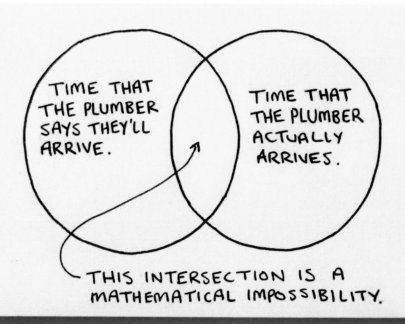

TIME THAT
THE PLUMBER
SAYS THEY'LL
ARRIVE.

TIME THAT
THE PLUMBER
ACTUALLY
ARRIVES.

THIS INTERSECTION IS A
MATHEMATICAL IMPOSSIBILITY.

If only baristas operated on the same laissez-faire attitude toward making coffee, then I could call work and tell them, "I'll be in sometime between 8 A.M. and 1 P.M., I'm just waiting for a coffee, really sorry, but it's the only time they can make it." Then I'd just hang out in the café all day, cursing baristas.

"Not doing stuff" is one of my favorite things to do on the weekends. It also means I'm unable to do a lot of other things because "not doing stuff" seems to take up a lot of my time. I'm very busy like that.

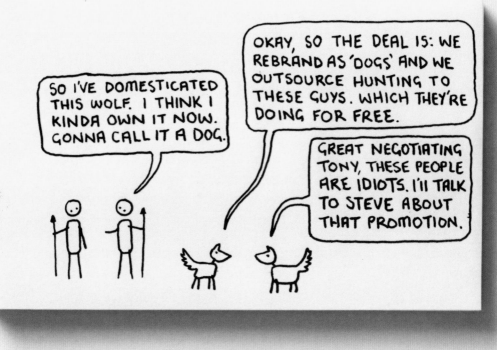

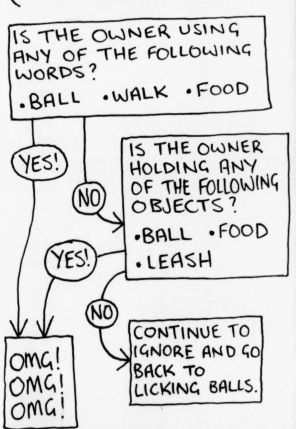

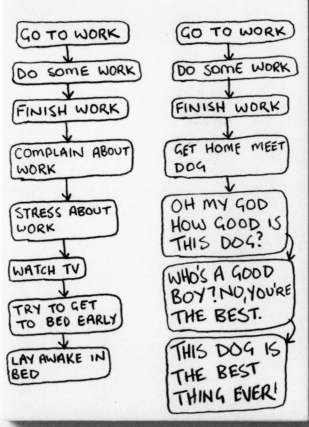

Sometimes I wonder if dogs actually love us, or if they've just realized that if someone follows you around and picks up your poo, then you shouldn't upset that person, because that is the behavior of someone who is clearly insane.

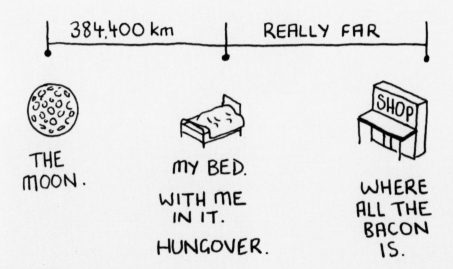

| 384,400 km | REALLY FAR |

THE MOON.

MY BED. WITH ME IN IT. HUNGOVER.

WHERE ALL THE BACON IS.

It took Neil Armstrong and Buzz Aldrin about eight days and close to 200 billion dollars in today's money to get to the moon and back, and after all that, they didn't even return with any bacon or delicious drinks. Which begs the question, just what *was* the point of going to the moon?

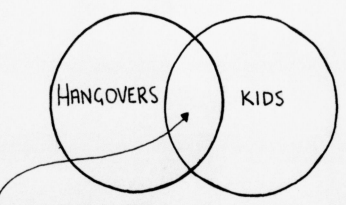

ANNOYING THINGS YOU HAVE TO LOOK AFTER ON A SUNDAY MORNING, BUT YOU CAN'T GET ANGRY WITH BECAUSE YOU MADE IT.

On the plus side, I've got great memories of my night out...
wait, no. No, I don't have those either.

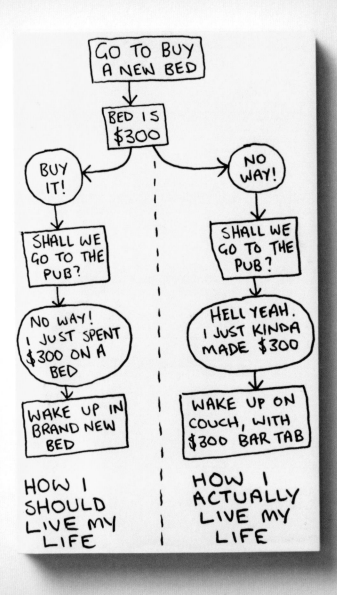

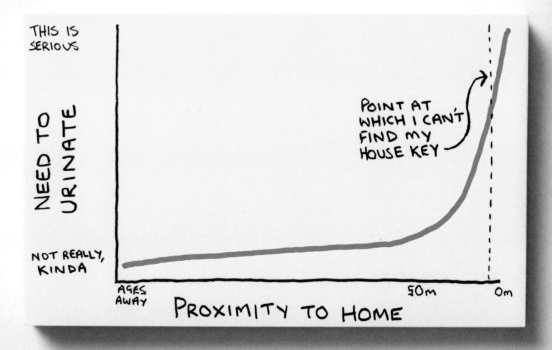

"Seriously Gary, reminding me that I should have gone when we were still at the pub is *not helping the situation right now*."

HOW THE ROOM LOOKED IN THE ADVERTISEMENT.

REALITY.

"Ah, OK. So that's just a painting of a window on the wall. And it's not actually a wall, but rather a curtain you've put up sectioning off a part of your living room. All of which makes your advertisement for this 'room' extremely misleading.

"However, I will obviously take it."

Can someone make an Ancestory.com for socks? I want to know what happened to the other half of my big old fluffy pair of sports socks. Where did it end up? Does it look to the sock drawer heavens each night, praying that one day it will be reunited with its mate, completely unaware that its match has since teamed up with another sock-widow and the two now make a very happy, albeit entirely odd, couple?

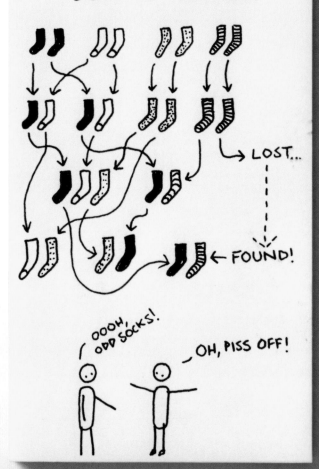

THIS SHOULD BE THE 'PROVE YOU'RE NOT A ROBOT' QUESTION...

 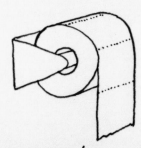

BECAUSE IF YOU DON'T KNOW WHICH ONE IS WRONG, THEN YOU HAVE NO SOUL.

And don't think I'm about to give you the answer. You'll just have to live your life knowing that there's a 50 percent possibility you're a robot.

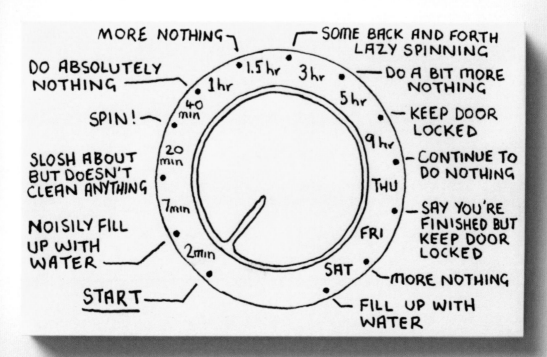

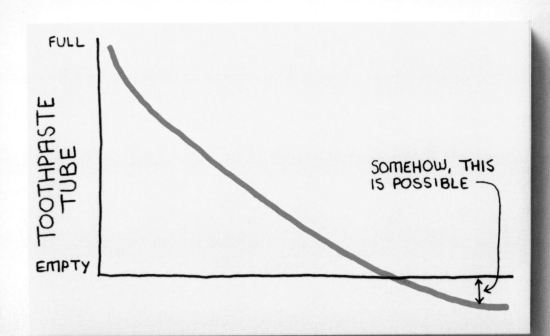

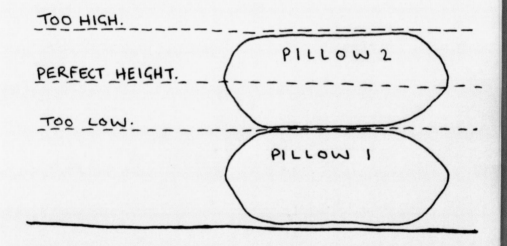

TOO HIGH.

PILLOW 2

PERFECT HEIGHT.

TOO LOW.

PILLOW 1

I'm now almost entirely convinced that this is just an ongoing joke in the design department at the pillow factory. Well played, pillow designers, well played.

Why does anyone bother with a wardrobe when you can utilize this far more ephemeral, fluctuating wardrobe that's less a physical object and more an obscure concept? It's certainly easier to put together than anything from Ikea.

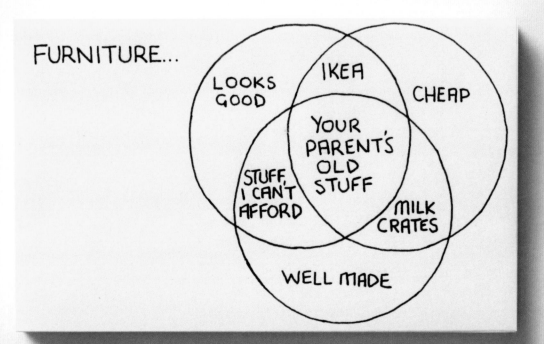

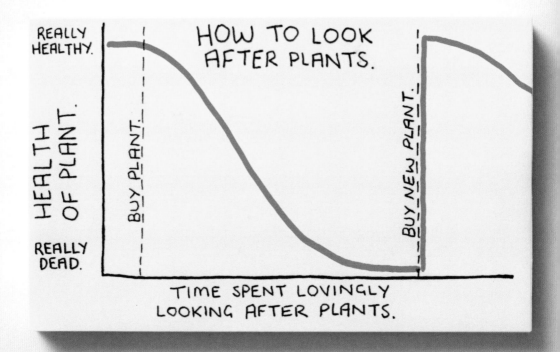

"Oh, you grow plants?"

"I prefer the term *caretaker*. I just make their lives comfortable before their imminent death."

ENTERTAINMENT

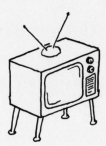

HOW TO BE CULTURED

TALK ABOUT GOING TO ART GALLERIES (YOU DON'T ACTUALLY HAVE TO GO).

DRINK RED WINE, PRETEND YOU CARE HOW IT TASTES.

READ A COMPLEX NOVEL UNTIL YOU FIND A PART YOU CAN REMEMBER, THEN TELL EVERYONE ABOUT IT.

PICK A THING, THEN PUT THE WORD 'POST' IN FRONT OF IT AND 'LANDSCAPE' AFTER IT. THEN USE THAT THREE-WORD PHRASE ALL THE TIME.

What the hell happened after Indiana Jones stole the idol? Were the owners compensated by the security guy? Did they leave a bad Yelp review? Did the fact that a U.S. archeology professor blatantly stole another country's priceless artifact at all affect the traditionally rocky bilateral relations between Peru and the United States? There are so many questions that *Raiders of the Lost Ark* failed to answer.

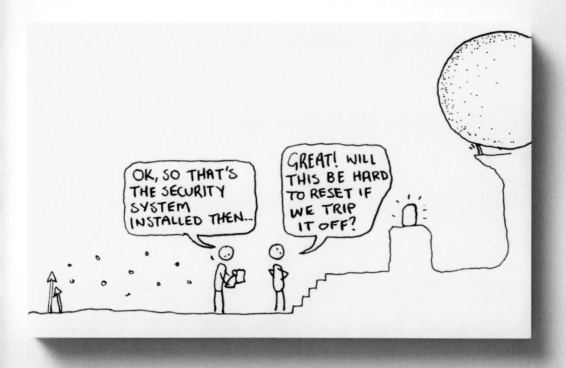

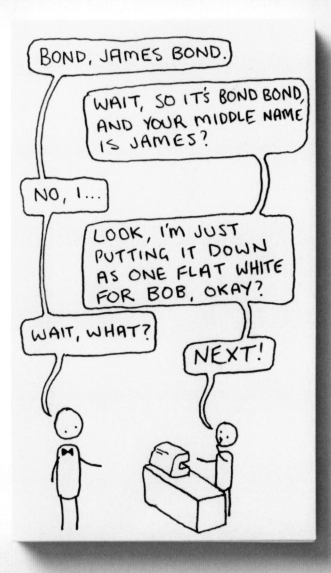

You see Bond drinking a lot of martinis, but you never see him struggling out of bed the next day and sucking down three espressos. There is no way you're getting up the next morning after even just two martinis and engaging in car chases and general badassery without a decent cup of coffee or two to get things going.

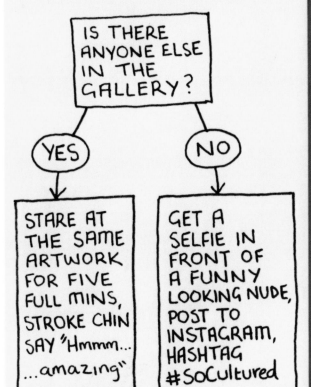

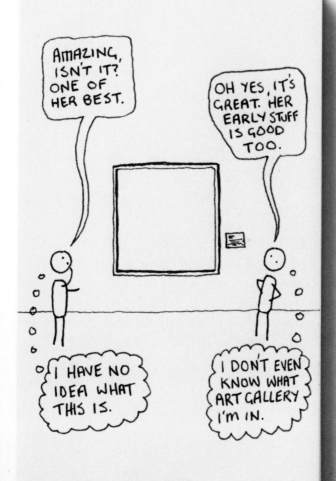

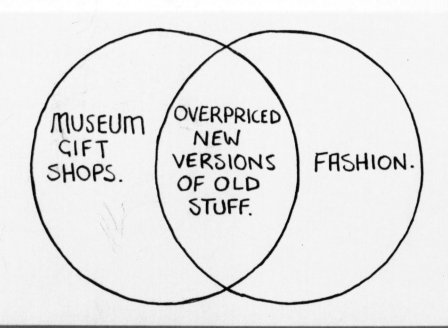

HOW TO WATCH A FILM AT THE CINEMA.

IDENTIFY SUPPORTING ACTORS.

REMEMBER OTHER FILMS THEY HAVE BEEN IN.

RELAY ALL THE ABOVE INFORMATION AS LOUD AS YOU CAN WHISPER TO THE PERSON NEXT TO YOU.

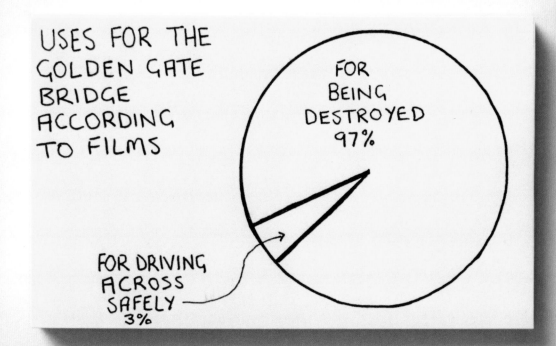

Al Zampa was a bridge builder who worked on many of the bridges around San Francisco. He is famous for surviving a fall off the Golden Gate Bridge during its construction. Al wasn't very good at dying, and he eventually lived to the ripe old age of ninety-five. There is even a bridge named in his honor, which, when you think about it, is a bit like naming a new species of shark after a shark-attack survivor.

USES FOR BASEMENTS OR ATTICS IN FILMS

HIDING FROM BAD THINGS

FINDING BAD THINGS

DOING BAD THINGS

A HANDY STORAGE SPACE

I'd love to see a scene in a film where someone goes into an attic or basement to retrieve something like their golf clubs or a box of VHS tapes and absolutely nothing happens while they're in there. And you know what? You'd still leave the cinema and say to your date, "Yeah, but that basement scene—what did it *really* mean?"

"I'm just going to go make some tea. Anyone want some tea? No? OK, I'll go make some tea."

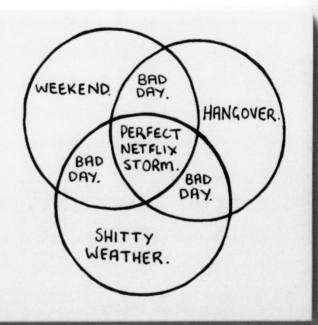

Sometimes three wrongs make a right.

You can actually watch Netflix trailers all day and never commit to anything, employing much the same attitude you have for your career. How great is that?

Sure, you could fill that void left by *House of Cards* with French lessons or pottery classes or completing an MBA. Or you could start scrolling through the uncharted backwaters of Netflix trying to find something, *anything* to watch, like the desperate TV-addicted junkie you are.

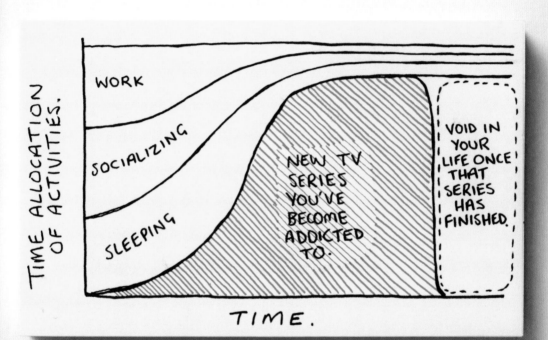

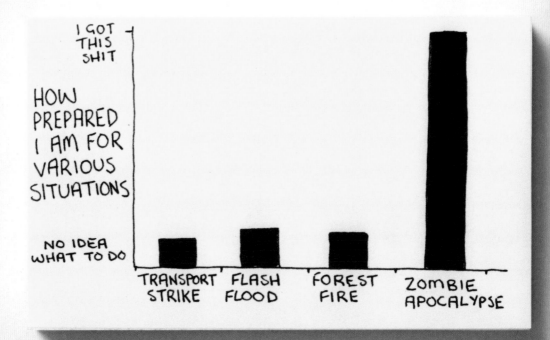

They're not zombie films, they're zombie *tutorials*.

THE REAL REASON LONG FLIGHTS ARE SCARY.

LIKELIHOOD THERE WILL ONLY BE AN ADAM SANDLER FILM LEFT TO WATCH.

LENGTH OF FLIGHT.

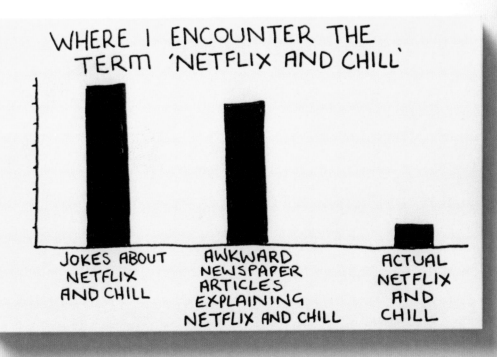

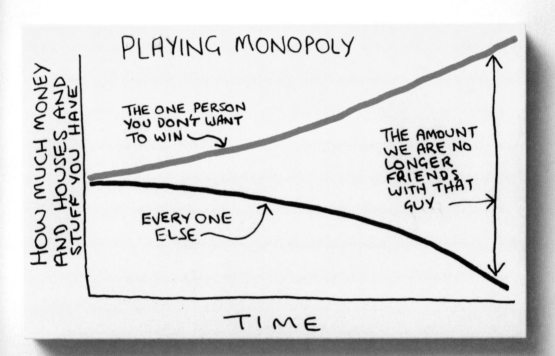

Twenties: "Guys, come on, there's nobody in here."

Thirties: "Guys, come on! There's nobody in here!"

Given that lines for bars are generally engineered by the bouncer to create the illusion of a wildly successful venue behind its closed doors, what you're really doing in that line is participating in a large-scale street performance art installation. So on the downside, you're an unwitting advertising tool, but on the upside, you're an artist.

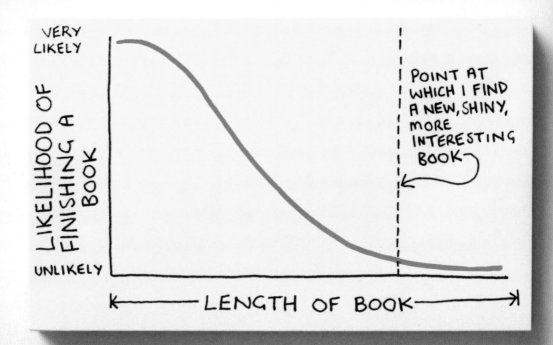

It's OK, I don't expect you to finish this one, either.

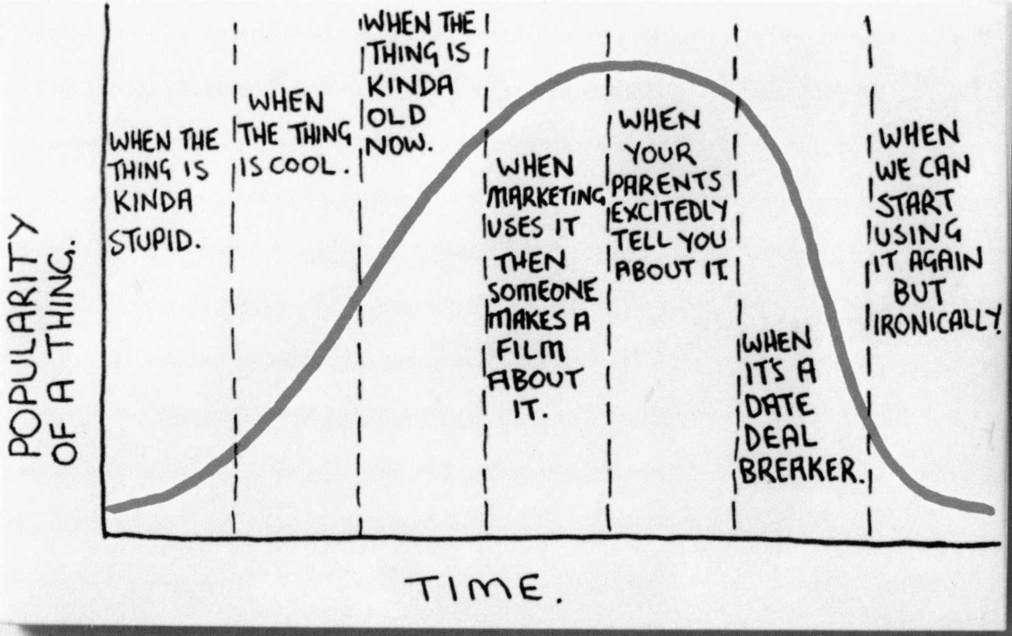
POPULARITY OF A THING.
WHEN THE THING IS KINDA STUPID.
WHEN THE THING IS COOL.
WHEN THE THING IS KINDA OLD NOW.
WHEN MARKETING USES IT THEN SOMEONE MAKES A FILM ABOUT IT.
WHEN YOUR PARENTS EXCITEDLY TELL YOU ABOUT IT.
WHEN IT'S A DATE DEAL BREAKER.
WHEN WE CAN START USING IT AGAIN BUT IRONICALLY.
TIME.

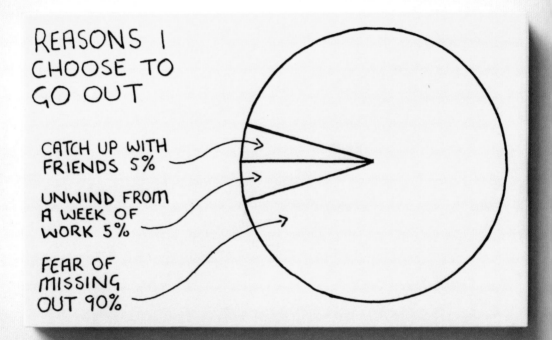

REASONS I CHOOSE TO GO OUT

CATCH UP WITH FRIENDS 5%

UNWIND FROM A WEEK OF WORK 5%

FEAR OF MISSING OUT 90%

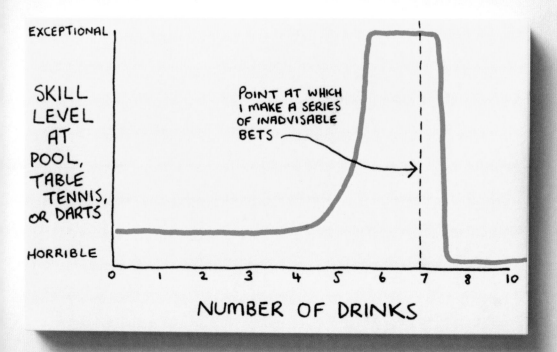

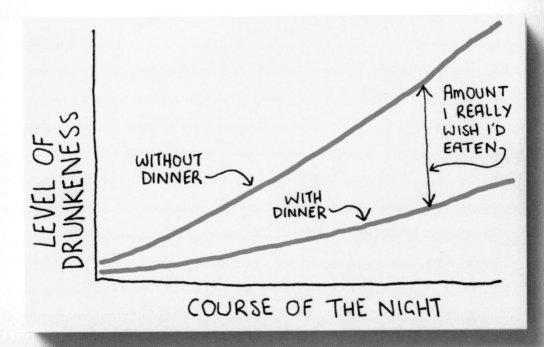

There's usually a short window to get this right, as it only takes about two and a half drinks to convince myself that a small bag of chips and a pint of Guinness is more or less the equivalent of a proper meal.

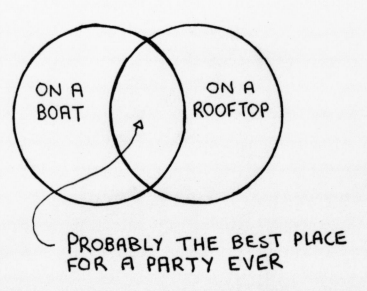

ON A
BOAT

ON A
ROOFTOP

PROBABLY THE BEST PLACE
FOR A PARTY EVER

Because there's nothing like the real chance of death by falling or
drowning to really kick a party into gear, right?

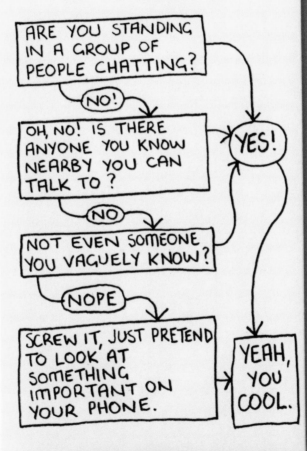

Once you've pretended to use your phone for longer than it takes to check your text messages, e-mail, Facebook, Twitter, Snapchat, Instagram, Tinder, and rate last night's Uber ride, you're going to need to leave.

5:30 P.M.: "We'll just have one or two, you know, nothing crazy—after all, we have that super important meeting tomorrow."

2:00 A.M.: "We didn't have anything important to do tomorrow, did we? I can't remember; I think it'll be fine, though. Shots for everyone!"

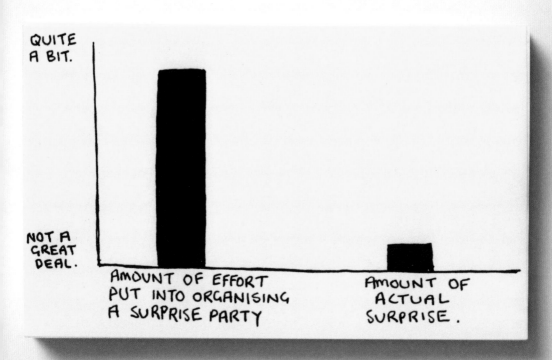

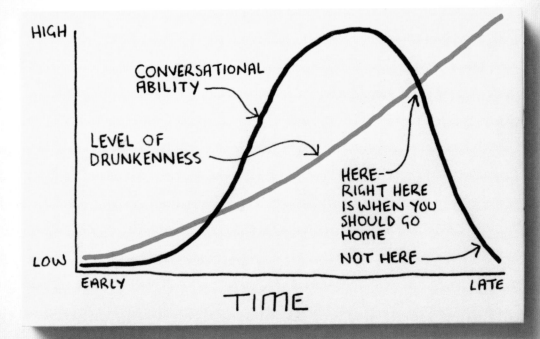

There's another line on this graph I could have drawn that starts quite high and gradually decreases, entitled, "Ability to realize the point at which I should go home." Who'd have thought going out could be so mathematically complicated?

WHAT PEOPLE
IMAGINE WHEN I
SAY I WAS THE
DJ AT A
HOUSE PARTY:

WHAT I WAS
ACTUALLY DOING
AT THE HOUSE
PARTY:

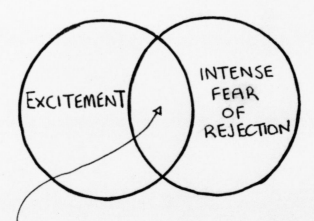

EXCITEMENT

INTENSE
FEAR
OF
REJECTION

WHEN YOUR REQUESTED SONG
FINALLY COMES ON

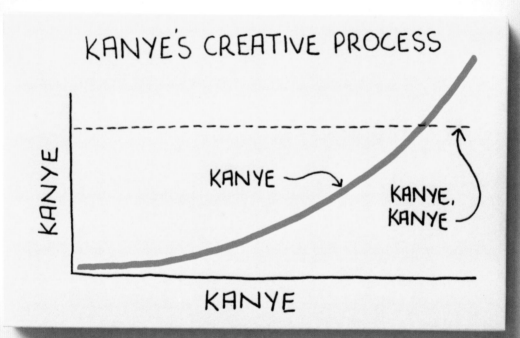

"I'm next to the guy with the hat! . . . No, not that hat, the other hat. . . . OK, see the red tent to the right of the stage? . . . OK, if you draw a line between the blue tent and the tree near the hat guy, then we're one third along that line but a little bit perpendicular to it. . . . No, you're thinking of parallel; perpendicular is like a right angle from the line. . . . Because perpendicular is a much better word! . . . OK, I'll just stay here until you happen to walk past us by chance."

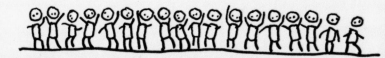

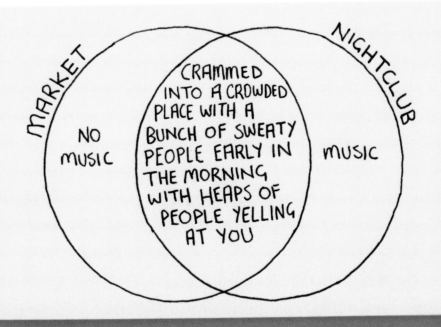

MARKET

NIGHTCLUB

NO MUSIC

CRAMMED INTO A CROWDED PLACE WITH A BUNCH OF SWEATY PEOPLE EARLY IN THE MORNING WITH HEAPS OF PEOPLE YELLING AT YOU

MUSIC

The difference between your twenties and thirties is really just a matter of location.

FRIEND WHO IS PRETENDING TO KNOW ABOUT WINE.

FRIEND WHO CAME IN LATE AND IS ALREADY QUITE DRUNK.

NEW BOYFRIEND THAT NOBODY KNOWS WHO'S KIND OF WEIRDING EVERYONE OUT.

FRIEND WHO JUST GOT IN FROM TRAVELING AND IS UNDER THE MISTAKEN IMPRESSION PEOPLE WANT TO HEAR THEIR STORIES.

WHO TO INVITE TO A DINNER PARTY.

FRIEND WHO INTERRUPTS ALL THE TIME WITH THEIR OWN VERSIONS OF THE SAME STORIES.

THE HOST WHO IS KIND OF REGRETTING ALL THIS.

FRIEND WHO WILL ARRIVE AT 11:30 PM, THINKING THIS WAS A HOUSE PARTY.

FRIEND WHO ONLY EVER REALLY TALKS ABOUT GAME OF THRONES.

"No, trust me, I'm quite happy doing the dishes."

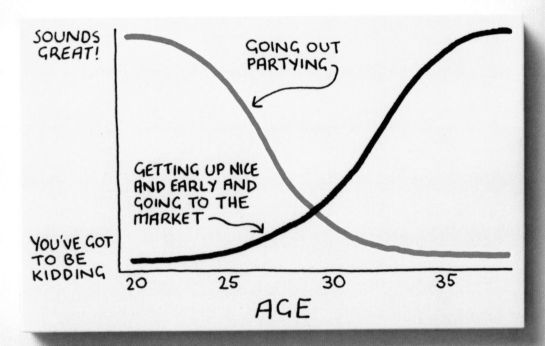

FOOD AND DRINK

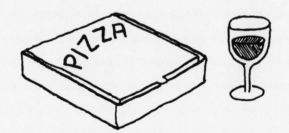

CHOOSING A PLACE
TO GO OUT TO
DINNER.

SOMEWHERE
CLOSE.

SOMEWHERE
NOT TOO
BUSY.

SOMEWHERE
NOT TOO
EXPENSIVE.

THIS PLACE DOESN'T
ACTUALLY EXIST.

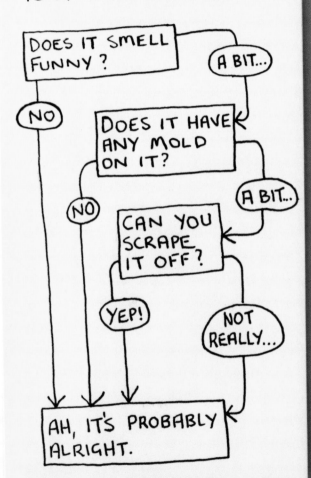

No, I don't know why I'm still single, either.

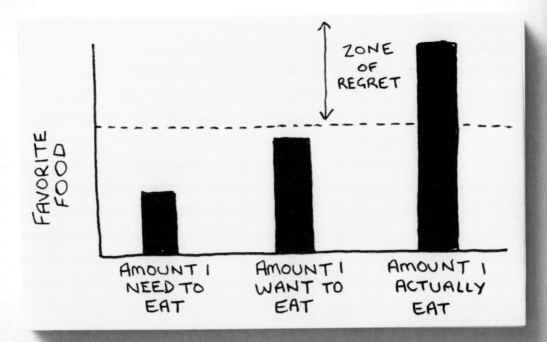

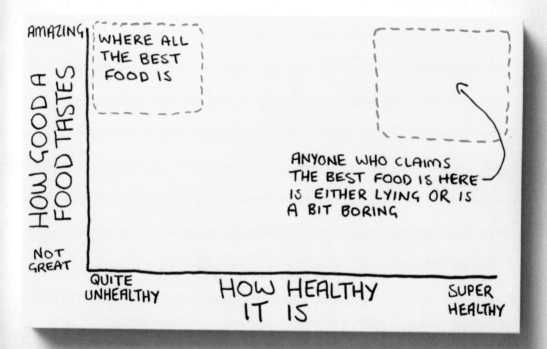

The fact that pizza is not a healthly food is perhaps the greatest proof that if God does exist, he enjoys a practical joke. "OK, watch me make half the planet obese."

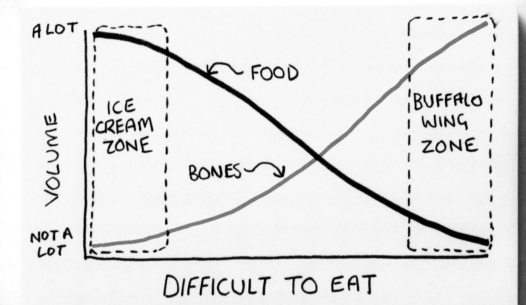

A local bar I used to frequent had a buffalo wing–eating challenge where the idea was to consume sixty buffalo wings within sixty minutes. People rarely finished them in the allotted time, and the record held at around fifty minutes for several years. Then one day a mysterious man arrived and left soon after, having set a record of sixteen minutes flat. He sat there in silence for the first twelve minutes, eating nothing, but systematically pulling the bones out of all the wings and placing them to the side until he had two piles, one of bones and one of all the chicken meat. He then proceeded to furiously consume the meat in just four spectacular minutes. He completely flipped the above chart on its head, and the entire spectacle still stands as the most ingenious and outright disgusting thing I have ever witnessed.

I have similar issues with "going to the gym."

HOW TO CHOOSE SOMETHING TO EAT FOR DINNER
WHILE AT WORK, THINK OF ALL THE DIFFERENT THINGS YOU COULD COOK...
GET HOME, ORDER TAKEAWAY

That moment when you think you've always known what you want, and it's time to finalize your decision. Then you realize—oh, no! Everything you thought you wanted was wrong, and you're going to have to start all over again, and you have no idea what to do, and you're pretty sure it's too late to start again.

No, I'm not talking about ordering in restaurants anymore. I'm talking about real life.

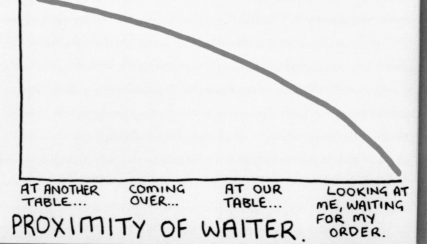

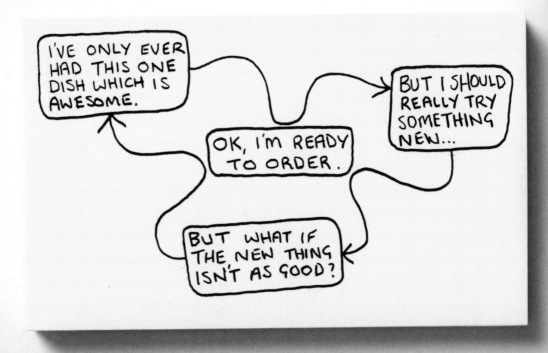

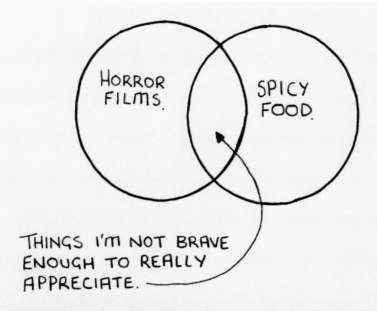

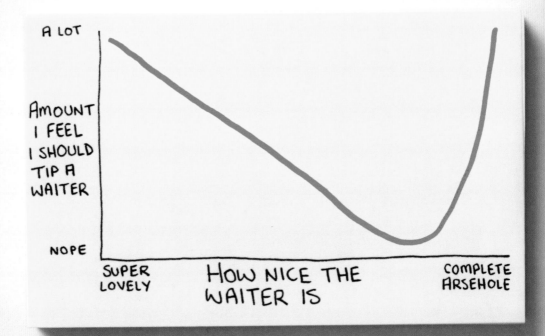

Trust me, we can buy their love.

I always get the portion size wrong, but I'm still too cautious to risk cooking too little. Is this another life metaphor I should take note of?

Clark Kent couldn't afford to be Superman today. Maybe it was possible back in the 1950s, when journalism paid, but these days he'd be too overworked to have time for fighting crime, and his paycheck wouldn't cover basic superhero expenses like suit repair, hair gel, and regular gym sessions. In real life, he'd have to get a second job at Whole Foods as an "avocado whisperer."

IF SUPERMAN REALLY DID EXIST.

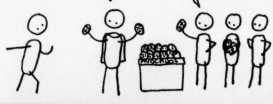

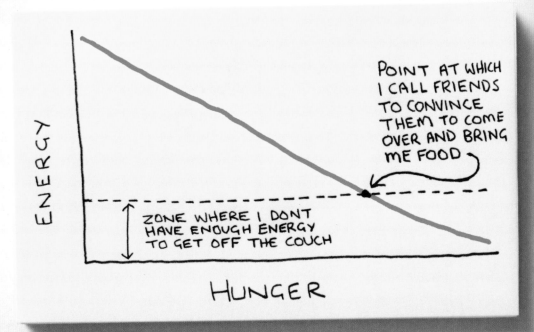

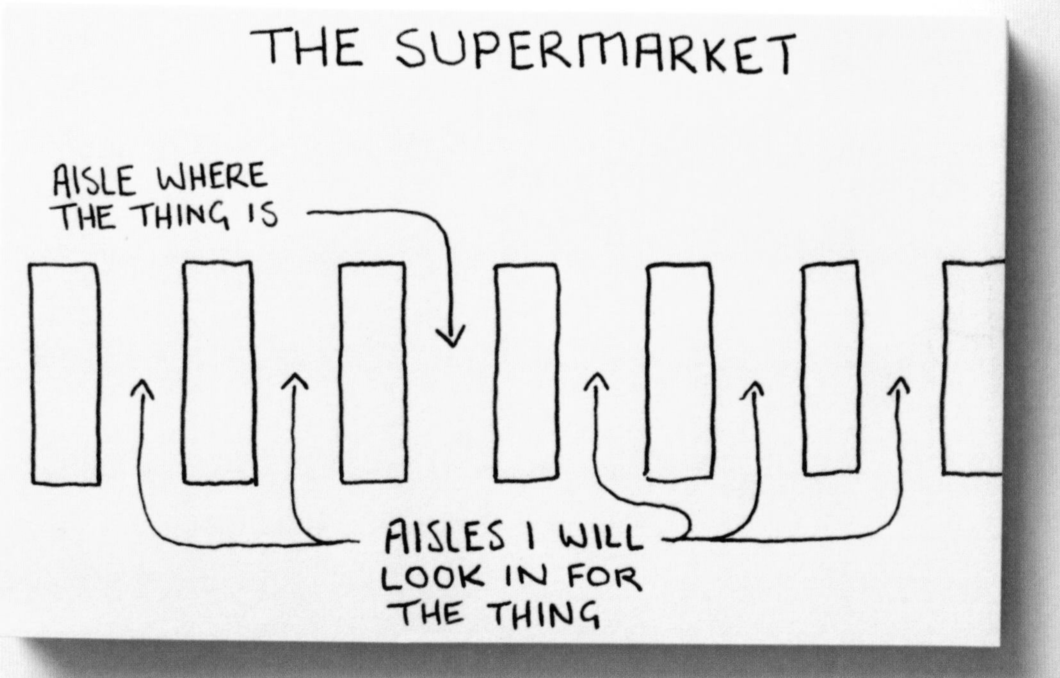
THE SUPERMARKET
AISLE WHERE THE THING IS
AISLES I WILL LOOK IN FOR THE THING

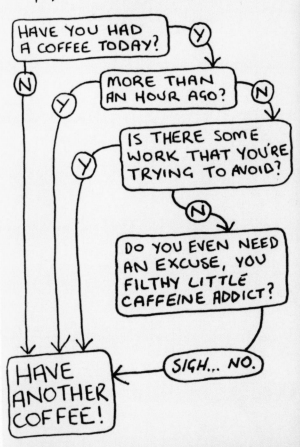

The only way I was able to write this book was due to a strict adherence to the logic of this chart.

People will tell you that green juice is better than coffee because it delivers a steadier energy release that is less likely to turn your kidneys inside out. However, these are the same people who will say that riding the teacups at the amusement park is just as thrilling as a roller coaster.

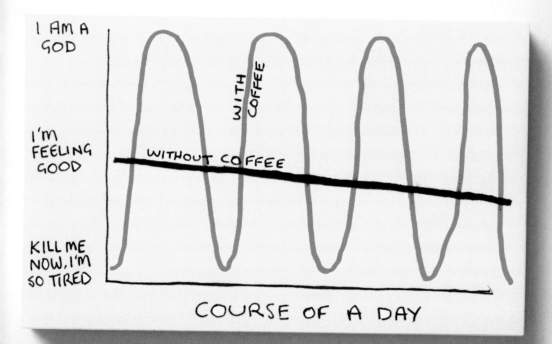

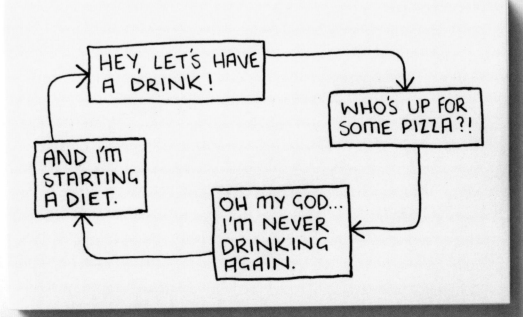

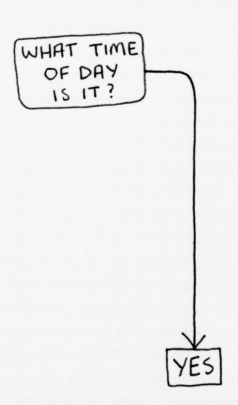

I'LL JUST HAVE A LITTLE GLASS TO REWARD MYSELF FOR MY NOT VERY HARD DAY AT WORK.
OKAY MAYBE TWO ... BIG ONES.
WHOA. THIS WINE GETS REALLY GOOD AFTER THREE.
ONE MORE. IT'S NOT LIKE I'M DRINKING THE ENTIRE BOTTLE.
THAT WOULD BE CRAZY...
KNOW WHAT'S NOT CRAZY? TEXTING MY EX. LET'S DO THAT!
OKAY, I NEED TO GET TO THE SHOP BEFORE THEY CLOSE.

As you move through your twenties, there are a few moments when you realize you're becoming an adult. For me, one was when I polished off a bottle of red while watching TV on a completely nondescript weeknight. Because if getting sloshed on your lonesome to forget your stressful day and answering to no one for that behavior isn't the most adult thing there is, I don't know what it could be.

Ironically, while martinis make you look quite classy, they also cause you to eventually look very, very, not classy.

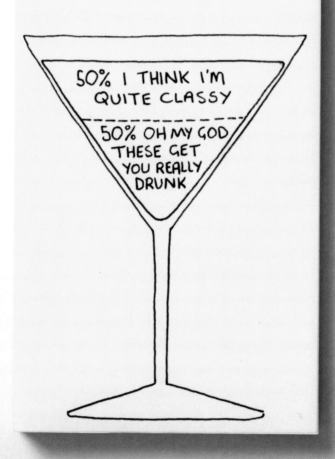

How to Choose Wine to Bring to Your Friends Dinner Party

GET ONE WITH A CORK BECAUSE YOU'RE CLASSY

GET THE 3rd CHEAPEST BOTTLE BECAUSE YOU'RE CHEAP BUT NOT *THAT* CHEAP

MAKE SURE THERE'S A PICTURE OF AN OLD BUILDING ON THE LABEL, THIS MEANS QUALITY

SAME WITH 'YE OLDE' WRITING

BE SURE TO PICK A LESSER KNOWN GRAPE VARIETY SO THE HOST CAN HOLD UP THE BOTTLE AND GO "OOOH! A GEWÜRZTRAMINER!"

I like how wine exists on a spectrum of sophistication. Sure, people scoff glasses of red while they swan around exhibition openings, but the homeless dude in the gutter outside the gallery is drinking wine, too. The trick is to be perfectly situated halfway between the two extremes.

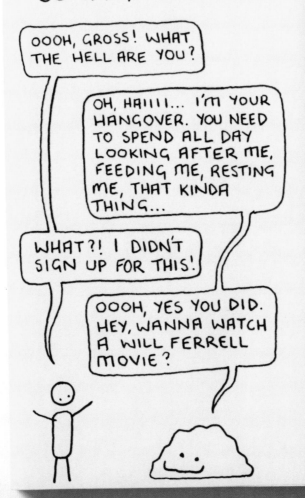

TECHNOLOGY

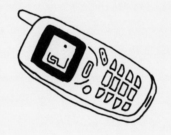

SHOULD YOU CALL OR TEXT?

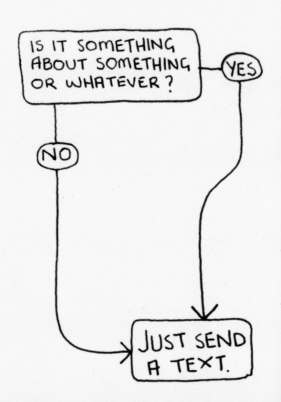

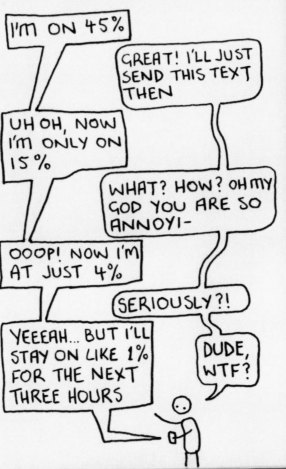

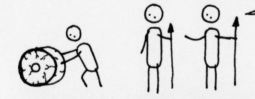

One day, the tide will turn, and all those people complaining that unnecessary phone use is rude will eventually die out, leaving us with the notion that *not* using your phone and just staring into space actually makes you look a little bit creepy.

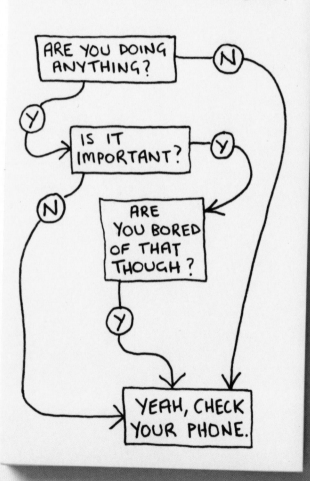

DAY 1: DOWNLOAD UBER.
COOL, THIS WILL BE HANDY WHEN THERE'S NO PUBLIC TRANSPORT OPTIONS.
DAY 14 OF USING UBER.
HEY, I'M JUST GOING TO THE CORNER STORE. WANNA COME?
YEP! HOLD ON...
OKAY. 'TONY' WILL BE HERE IN 3 MINUTES.

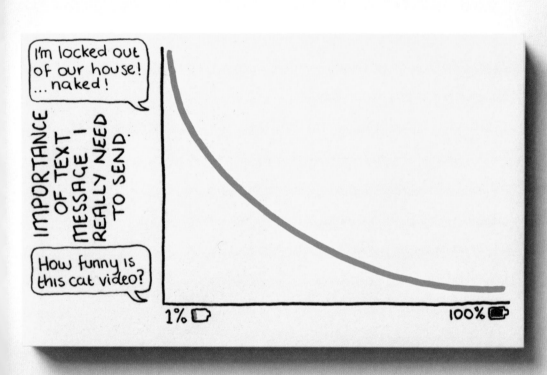

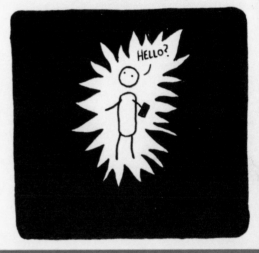

In 1915, Ernest Shackleton and a crew of twenty-seven men set out to cross Antarctica. Their ship, *Endurance*, was eventually trapped in sea ice, and they survived the winter before the ship finally sank, stranding the men on the ice with no chance of rescue. They then drifted on ice for a few more months before getting back into small boats as the ice melted, eventually arriving at the uninhabited Elephant Island. From there, Shackleton and four others made an 800 mile sea journey in a small open boat and then trekked over a mountainous island to finally find help.

Thankfully, Shackleton died long before he could suffer the much worse fate of a dead phone battery on a Saturday night.

In Stanley Kubrick's 1968 film *2001: A Space Odyssey*, the main protagonist makes a video call from an orbiting space station to his daughter on Earth. The scene is designed to show how advanced the future would be. However, if the film had been an accurate prediction, his daughter would have screamed into the phone, *"I've told you not to video call me, Dad!"* This indicates that Kubrick completely misjudged mankind's relationship with technology, which is quite ironic.

THE PAST
IN THE FUTURE, WE'LL BE ABLE TO TALK FACE-TO-FACE ON SMALL HAND HELD DEVICES.
WHOA! COOL.
THE FUTURE
AAAGH! IT'S ON FACE-TIME!!
TURN IT OFF! TURN IT OFF!

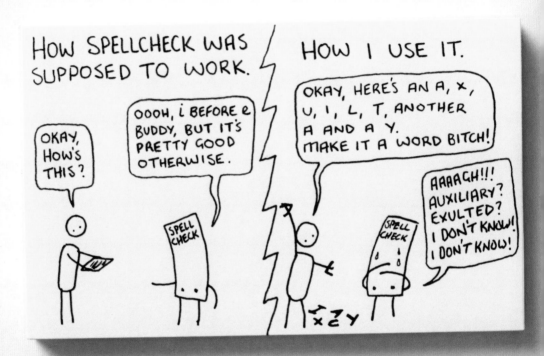

HOW PEOPLE USE A GOPRO IN ADS FOR GOPRO.

PARACHUTE

GOPRO

GNARLY WAVE

ON FIRE

ROCKS

SHARK

HOW PEOPLE ACTUALLY USE A GOPRO.

UM... WHY IS OUR DOG WEARING A GOPRO?

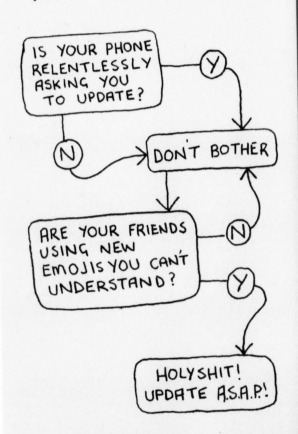

The terrifying reason I avoid downloading updates is because when your phone is out of action for forty-five minutes, there's nothing to stop the existential dread that seeps in and washes over you in the interim, reminding you that you're ultimately alone and you can't possibly cope within this vacuum.

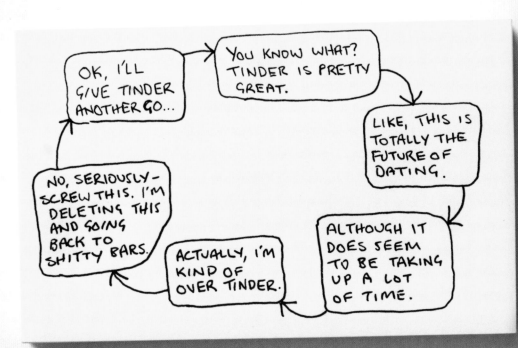

Online dating is basically the equivalent of walking into a room full of strangers and telling all the ones you find unattractive to leave. About a quarter of the people remaining in the room ask how your Monday was and another quarter say some weird creepy stuff, so you tell all of them to leave as well. Then you talk to the remainder, who all turn out to be way too into martial arts or think Coldplay is the height of musical achievement, at which point you decide it's all too hard. So you leave the room and go read a book and think about how having a cat and being alone forever is actually quite good.

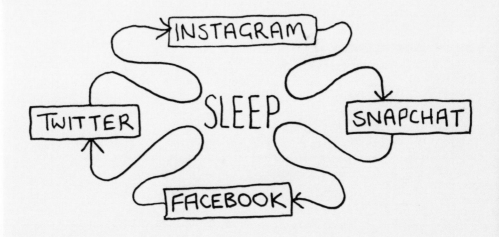

Eventually, I'll complete a lap where I don't encounter any new notifications, and then, and *only then*, will I sleep.

Some people wonder when the robots will take over but I've got a sneaking suspicion it'll be when the last human is finally locked out of the Internet.

Instalkerphobia

noun.

1. THE INTENSE FEAR THAT YOUR FRIEND WILL ACCIDENTALLY DOUBLE TAP WHILE THEY'RE USING YOUR PHONE TO LOOK AT THE PERSON YOU'VE GOT A CRUSH ON.

Friend: "What? You can't zoom? Oh, sorry."

Me: [*walks into ocean*]

CLIMATE CHANGE

MY PARENTS FORGETTING THEIR PASSWORDS

THINGS THAT ARE PROBABLY GOING TO KEEP HAPPENING DESPITE EVERYONES BEST INTENTIONS

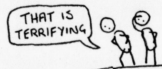

ASSORTED
NONSENSE

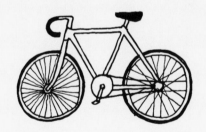

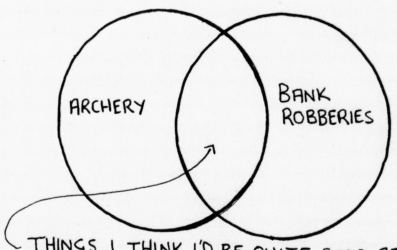

ARCHERY

BANK ROBBERIES

THINGS I THINK I'D BE QUITE GOOD AT BUT FOR VARIOUS REASONS NEVER TRY OUT

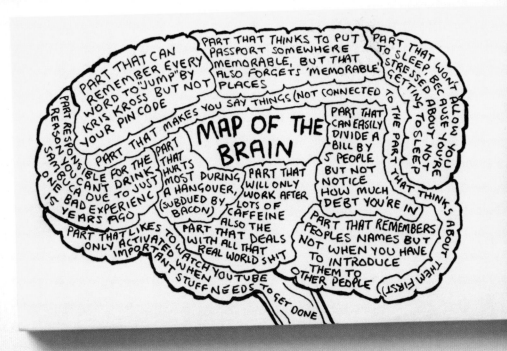

A neuroscientist told me this map "looks about right," which either means I've somehow just guessed what's going on in a brain or neuroscientists have a worryingly broad definition of what counts as "about right."

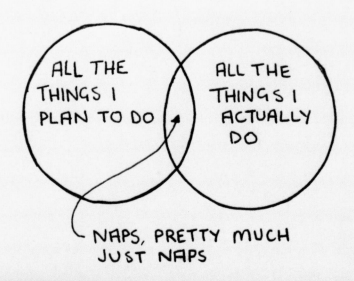

If I'm completely honest, naps come under "things I didn't plan to do," as well.

WHAT ALL MY 'TO-DO' LISTS ULTIMATELY LOOK LIKE.
1. write numbered 'TO-do' list with checkboxes and everything.
2. do all the stuff I need to do.
3. finish off with a glass of wine.

"We should probably itemize all the drinks individually so the list looks a bit more impressive, right?"

IF I WAS A SUPERHERO.

THANK GOD YOU GOT HERE 'BRUTALLY HONEST MAN' THERE'S PEOPLE THAT NEED SAVING!

DON'T THANK GOD, YOU CAN THANK OUR SEVERELY UNDERFUNDED PUBLIC TRANPORT SYSTEM.

ALSO, I DON'T THINK I CAN HELP, I'M NOT ACTUALLY VERY GOOD AT THIS KIND OF THING.

ALSO, HORRIBLE TIE.

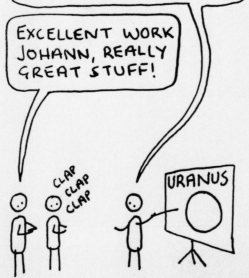

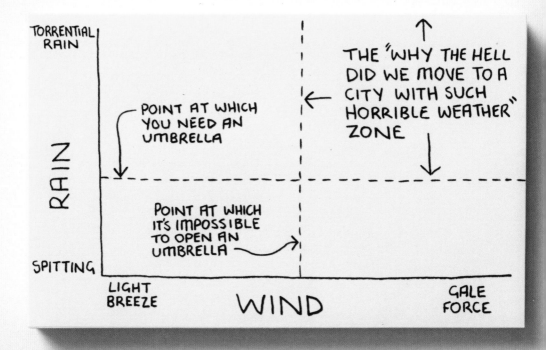

I love how the two things that are key to life on earth are air and water, yet when it comes to living on earth, these are the two things we generally complain about the most.

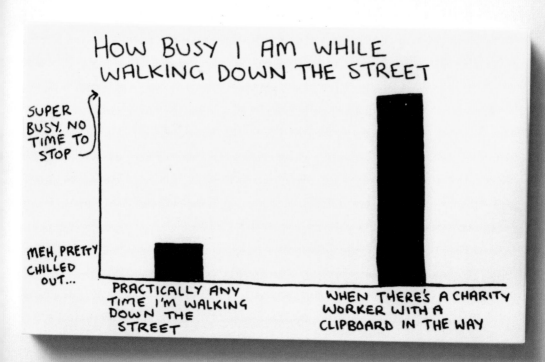

HOW TO IDENTIFY A HIPSTER.
ARE THEY DRESSED SLIGHTLY DIFFERENTLY FROM YOU?
A BIT, YEAH
OMG, TOTALLY A HIPSTER.

You might think someone's a hipster, but that person thinks someone else is a hipster, and someone, somewhere, thinks you're a hipster. "Hipster" is just a relative concept most often deployed to reconcile that we're all a little bit different. And actually, everyone is usually quite nice if you take the time to say hello and compliment his or her ridiculous hat.

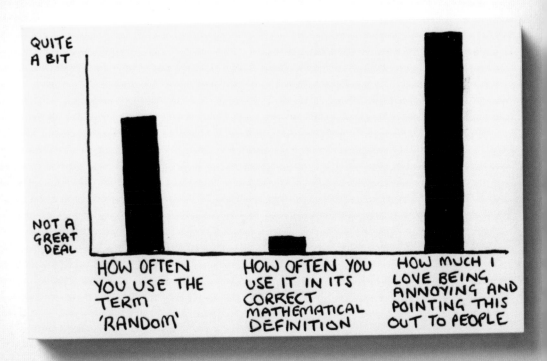

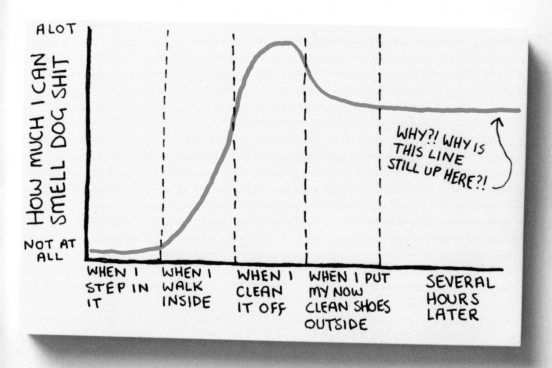

They say when you lose a limb you can still feel it. I feel like dog turds inspire exactly the same phenomenon.

THOUGHT PROCESS WHILE TELLING AN HILARIOUS STORY

THESE PEOPLE ARE GOING TO LOVE THIS STORY.

I WILL BE QUITE POPULAR AFTERWARDS.

WAIT, WHY DIDN'T ANYONE LAUGH AT THAT FIRST BIT?

OH GOD, I GOT THIS WRONG. THIS ISN'T FUNNY AT ALL.

ABORT! TAKE IT IN A DIFFERENT DIRECTION!

SHIT! THIS IS EVEN LESS FUNNY THAN BEFORE.

YOU'RE GOING TO HAVE TO DEPLOY THE "GUESS YOU HAD TO BE THERE" LINE...

...UNLESS, YOU TURN THIS INTO A FART JOKE. YEAH, YOU GOT THIS CHAZ.

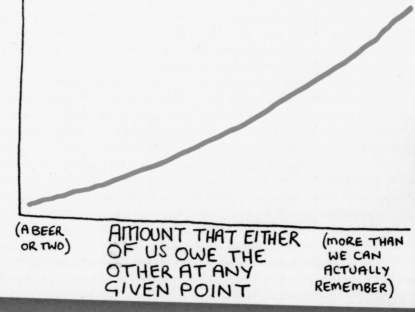

STRENGTH OF FRIENDSHIP

(A BEER OR TWO)

AMOUNT THAT EITHER OF US OWE THE OTHER AT ANY GIVEN POINT

(MORE THAN WE CAN ACTUALLY REMEMBER)

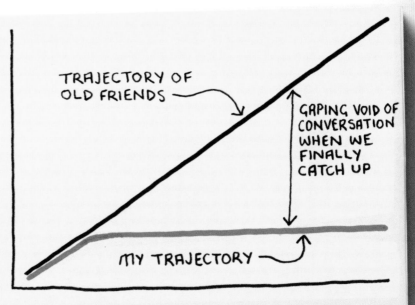

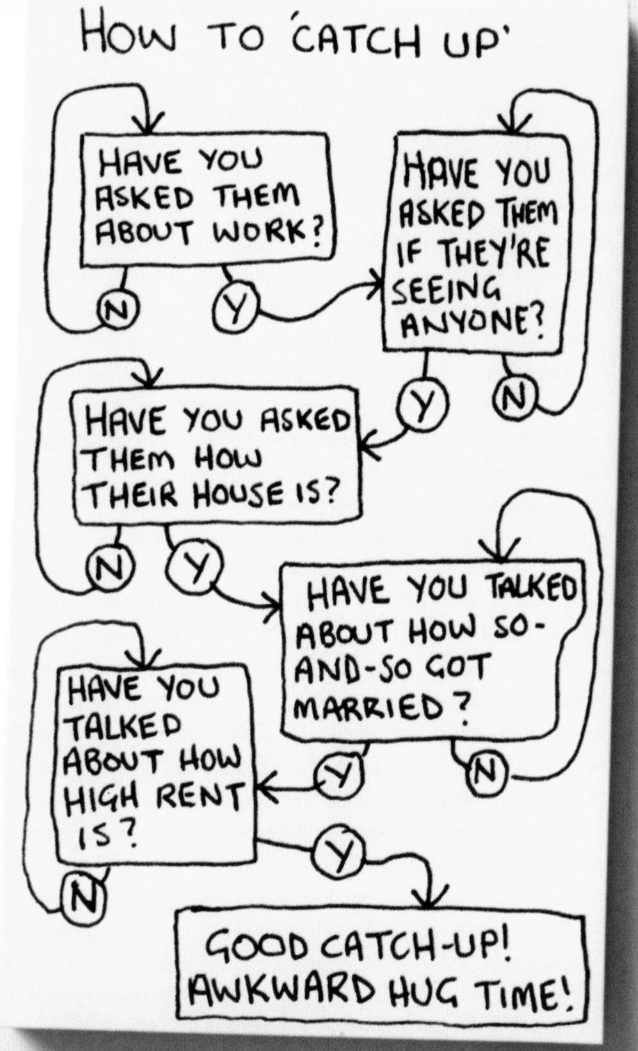
HOW TO 'CATCH UP'
HAVE YOU ASKED THEM ABOUT WORK?
N
Y
HAVE YOU ASKED THEM IF THEY'RE SEEING ANYONE?
Y
N
HAVE YOU ASKED THEM HOW THEIR HOUSE IS?
N
Y
HAVE YOU TALKED ABOUT HOW SO-AND-SO GOT MARRIED?
Y
N
HAVE YOU TALKED ABOUT HOW HIGH RENT IS?
Y
N
GOOD CATCH-UP! AWKWARD HUG TIME!

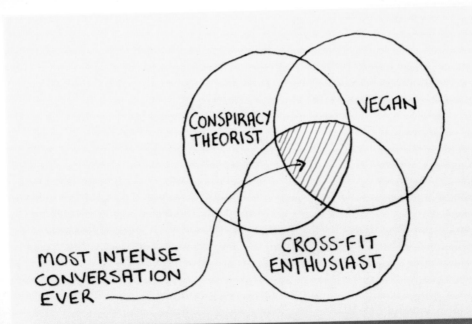

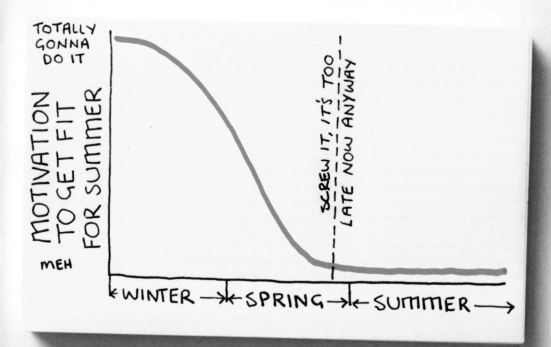

Plan B: buy a whole new wardrobe and instead of being fit, just concentrate on looking utterly fabulous.

GYM MOTIVATION VENN DIAGRAM
TIMES THAT I AM MOTIVATED TO GO TO THE GYM.
TIMES THAT I AM ABLE TO GO TO THE GYM.

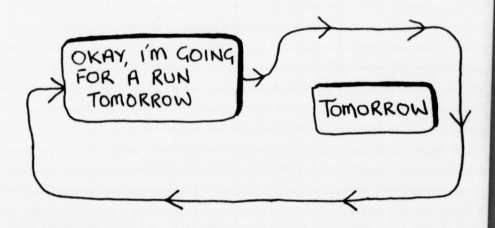

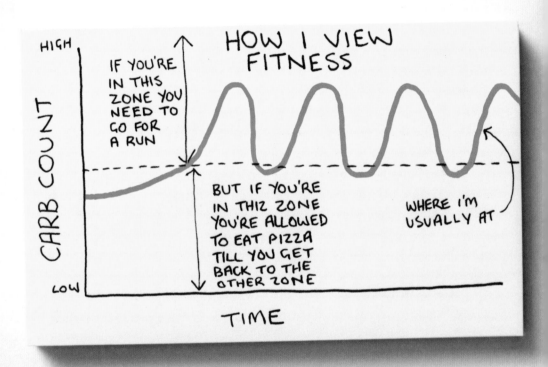

The amount of calories you burn walking to the fridge totally justifies all the bacon you take out of it. At least that's what helps *me* sleep.

This completely flips if you've just run a marathon, in which case you'll no doubt be talking about that a lot.

THE MATHS:

RATE OF HUMAN HAIR GROWTH : 15cm per YEAR.

AVERAGE AGE OF DAMSEL-IN-DISTRESS (ACCORDING TO HOLLYWOOD) : 22 YEARS OLD.

THEREFORE: RAPUNZEL'S TOWER IS, AT MOST, JUST OVER 3 METERS TALL.

There's a good chance Rapunzel quite liked living with her folks and just made up the "trapped in a tower" thing as a good excuse for why she hadn't bothered moving out to live with a dodgy roommate. I don't blame her, either. It's tough for Generation Y to support themselves, so kudos to you if you can cook up an elaborate story that saves on rent and bags you a prince in the process.

SCHRÖDINGER'S CAVITY.

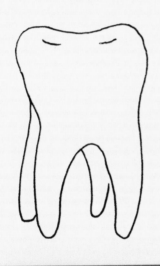

IT *COULD* BE A CAVITY,
BUT UNTIL YOU SEE A
DENTIST, IT COULD ALSO
NOT BE A CAVITY.

THEREFORE, NOT SEEING A
DENTIST GIVES IT THE
GREATEST CHANCE OF IT
NOT BEING A CAVITY.

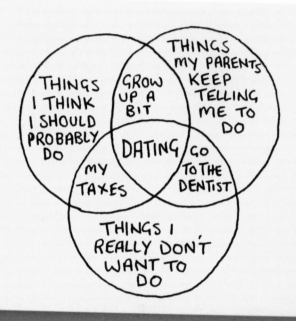

"No, Mom, I haven't tried dating a dentist yet."

Say what you will about arranged marriages, but at least they didn't have the hassle of choosing the perfect place for a date.

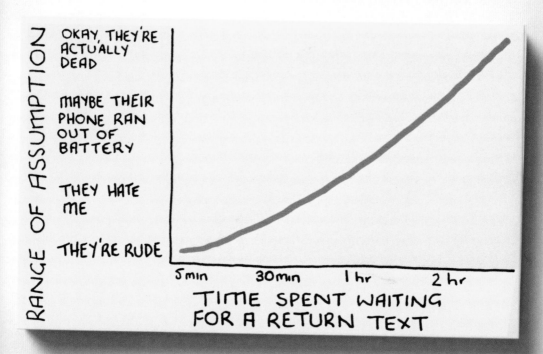

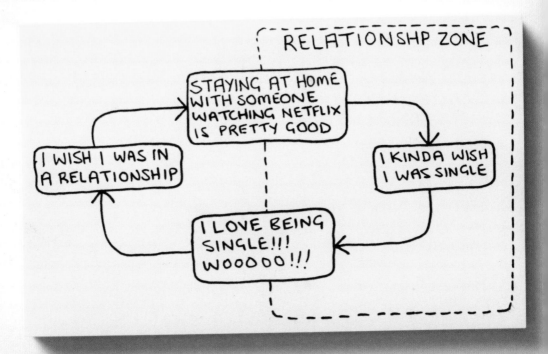

My father used to tell me that "the grass is always greener on the other side of the fence," but he is a farmer, so it's hard to know if he was offering up poignant advice or literally talking about grass and fences.

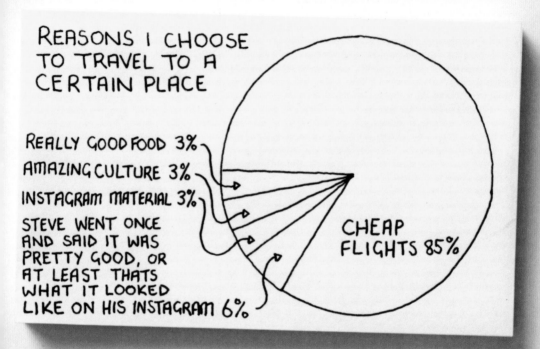

REASONS I CHOOSE TO TRAVEL TO A CERTAIN PLACE

REALLY GOOD FOOD 3%
AMAZING CULTURE 3%
INSTAGRAM MATERIAL 3%
STEVE WENT ONCE AND SAID IT WAS PRETTY GOOD, OR AT LEAST THATS WHAT IT LOOKED LIKE ON HIS INSTAGRAM 6%

CHEAP FLIGHTS 85%

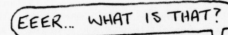
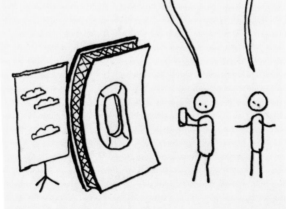

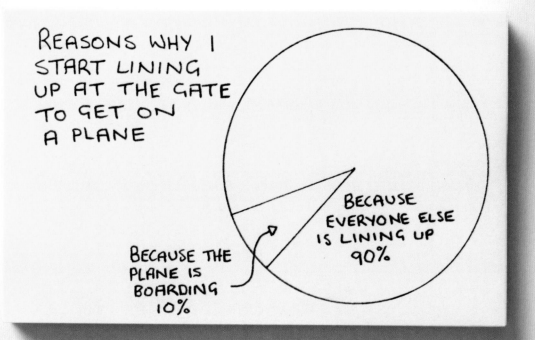

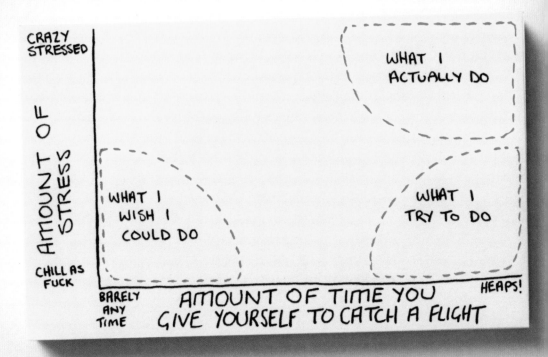

Wake up at the time I intended. Realize that in retrospect, it might not have been early enough. Get the train to the airport. Train is on time, but I suspect it's going slower than usual, so I begin to panic. Arrive at the airport, horrified to discover a long, snaking line moving slowly through security. Begin *really* panicking. Formulate ways to jump the line without looking like someone who shouldn't be let on a flight. Begin profusely sweating. Observe customs official giving me that suspicious look they reserve for obvious drug traffickers. Finally and miraculously clear customs. Run to the gate while freaking out. *I'm going to miss this flight, how did I get this so wrong?!*

Arrive at the gate with a full hour and a half to spare.

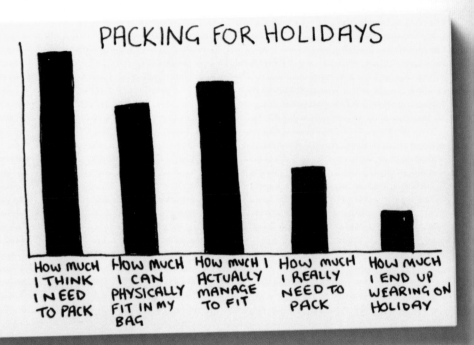

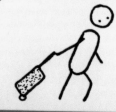

Lately I've been changing it up a bit and scaring the hell out of my friend's adolescent children: "So Johnny, what drugs are the kids at school doing these days?"

Would you like to withdraw cash? Yes.
Would you like to check your balance? No.

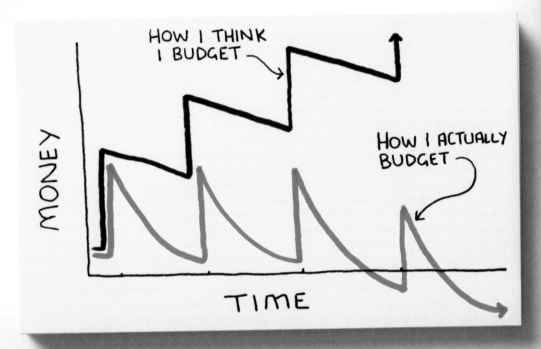

"How hard is it to sell your own kidneys?"

I assume a good understanding of this kind of thing occurs the same way gray or receding hair does—generally against your will, and just in time to be taken seriously as an adult.

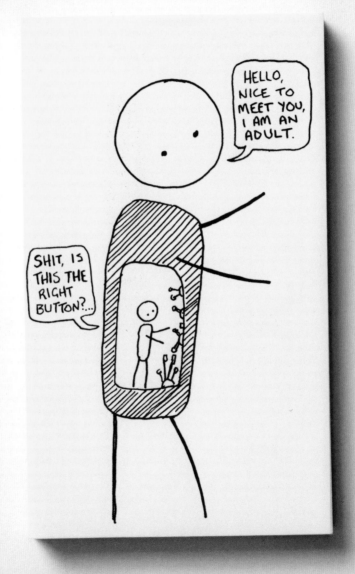

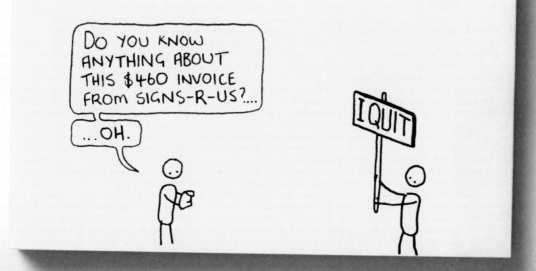

This has been a (mostly) true story.

ACKNOWLEDGEMENTS

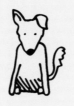

There are quite a few people without whom this project would not have happened.

I should probably thank Spencer Silver and Arthur Fry, cocreators of the sticky note, not to mention Ryosuke Namiki and Masao Wada, cofounders of the Pilot Corporation, producers of the Pilot Fineliner, the most hardworking pen in my arsenal and my comedic weapon of choice. Also, Tim Berners-Lee, and whoever invented Instagram, I guess.

However, my biggest thanks go to the members of a group message thread where I first began to post these drawings. Over several months they convinced me to put them onto the Internet. I repeatedly told them it was a terrible idea and nothing would come of it, and I've never been happier to be proven wrong. Gal, Pav, Fi, Rin—thank you a million times over.

Thank you to my amazing parents, who dealt with their son throwing away a career in architecture to draw idiotic things on sticky notes not just well, but were also exceedingly supportive of the idea. To Sis and Lib, thank you for all your drawing ideas and for generally being the best sisters ever. And to my incredible grandfather Paps—our countless lunches could provide enough material for a book in its own right.

Thanks to my agents, Christopher and Nicola, without whom I'd have no idea what I was doing.

Thanks to David and the lovely folks at Abrams for expertly turning an Internet thing into an actual physical object and making sure all my weird Australian humor makes sense to an American audience.

To everyone in the "Eurovision Warehouse" that's been my home and studio for the last year: Huw, Bremond, Josie, Anna, Marjut, Lior, and Talia, thank you for respectively giving your English, French, German, Polish, Finnish, and Israeli per-

spectives on all my jokes, as well as countless meals, drinks, and general fun times. (An extra special thanks to Anna for her photography skills.)

Thanks to everyone I used to work with in architecture who didn't seem to mind that I spent most of the time drawing comics and wasting time on the Internet rather than drawing buildings. You know who you are.

London friends and lovers: Sophie Caroline Jepson for your incredible word generation skills; Lee-wah, Katie, JC, Scotty, Wakes, Pip, and the rest of the Aussie contingent; the entire Russell family for being my away-from-home pseudo-family; and of course, Mr. Hope, both friend and begrudging patron—thank you.

To Stoke Newington's finest: The guy who runs my local corner store for keeping up the avocado supply; the Good Egg for making the best breakfast and coffee in London; Original Sin for supplying all the pool and drinks a man could ever want— thank you.

Australian friends from home whose friendships have provided a lot of the material in this book: Trigger and Alice, Glenn, Mr. Dan Salmon (and your excellent comedic brain), Georgia, Hugh and Tanja, Ange, and of course the best dog in the world, #BarryWiegard.

And obviously, thank you to (at last count) 136,000 people following the @instachaaz Instagram account. Without all those follows and comments and likes, this entire project would still be a little known procrastination tool that I would have lost interest in by now. The collective weight of this following served as proof that the Instagram collection might work as a book. So without all of you, nobody would have discovered it, especially the kind of people who turn these types of things into books. Thank you, thank you, thank you.